My First Book on
SIKHISM

DIVINITY
(Sikh Studies Book-1)

The Sikh Gurus, Shrines, Symbols, Personages, Practices and Festivals

Hemkunt

Note for the Teachers and Parents

Understanding different religions and the basic elements underlying them, lays the foundation for a good human being. Such understanding must be imparted at an early age.

Keeping this in view, Sikh Public Schools in India have introduced religious instruction known as 'Sikh Studies' or 'Divinity' as a compulsory part of their curriculum. The present series has been developed to provide them a complete course in the subject upto the secondary stage.

The series is also aimed at meeting the needs of Sikh children settled abroad by giving them graded tools for study at home or in a Sunday school. This will also be a good resource material for use in summer camps for Sikh children studying in other schools.

The series consists of the following books:

Book I-II are meant as a launching pad for a study of Sikhism by junior children. They cover the basic facts about Sikhism for beginners. As reading skills are being developed at this stage, illustrations are profusely given to be used as a fulcrum. We also solicit the support of parents and teachers for imparting knowledge. Hints for them have been given at the end of each chapter.

Book III-V give *sakhis* or stories about the Sikh Gurus. They have become a part of the folklore in Punjab. They most effectively convey the teachings of Sikhism in a manner traditionally accepted in all religions.

Book VI gives similar *sakhis* or stories about the Sikh Heroes. It thus covers the post-Guru Gobind Singh period of Sikh History. In fact it carries Sikh history, from Banda Singh Bahadur to Maharaja Ranjit Singh.

Book VII is a formal culmination of the series for adolescent children. It introduces them formally to Sikh theology, ethics, psyche etc. after tracing the evolution of Sikhism.

Supplementary Book. It gives the complete *Ardaas* with pictorial cues for easy learning. The text is given in both Gurmukhi and Roman scripts with an English translation.

We have tried to keep the language as simple as possible. But there are obvious limitations because of the nature of the subject matter. We hope that illustrations will relieve this feature to some extent. Comments and suggestions for improvement are welcome.

– Authors

CONTENTS

THE SIKH GURUS
Guru Nanak Dev

Guru Nanak Dev is the first Guru of the Sikhs. He is the founder of Sikh religion. He said all the people are children of one God. He started the practice of Langar.

Hints for Parents and Teachers :

Explain Guru Nanak Dev's attitude towards equality of all men by starting the tradition of religious congregation and *langar*. He did not believe in any rituals. Tell the story about his refusal to wear 'sacred thread' and his throwing water in the opposite direction at Hardwar.

Guru Angad Dev

Guru Angad Dev is the second Guru of the Sikhs. He was a disciple of Guru Nanak Dev. He spread Guru Nanak Dev's teachings.

Guru Amardas

Guru Amardas is the third Guru of the Sikhs. He was a disciple of Guru Angad. He spread teachings of Guru Nanak. He carried on the tradition of Langar.

Hints for Parents and Teachers :

Tell the story of Akbar who took *langar* at Goindwal when he came to meet Guru Amardas.

Guru Ramdas

Guru Ramdas is the fourth Guru of the Sikhs. He founded the city of Amritsar. He was a disciple and son-in-law of Guru Amardas. He spread Sikhism in north India.

Hints for Parents and Teachers :

It would be interesting to tell the children the story of Amritsar which grew into a city over the years around '*Amrit Sarovar*' and thus how it got its name.

Guru Arjan Dev

Guru Arjan Dev is the fifth Guru of the Sikhs. He was the youngest son of Guru Ramdas. The building of the Golden Temple was started by him. Guru Granth Sahib was also compiled by him.

Guru Hargobind

Guru Hargobind is the sixth Guru of the Sikhs. He was the only son of Guru Arjan Dev. The Moghul kings were forcing people to become Muslims. The Guru fought against this. He got the Akal Takhat built at Amritsar.

Guru Har Rai

Guru Har Rai is the seventh Guru of the Sikhs. He was the grandson of Guru Hargobind. He made Sikhism strong and popular.

Hints for Parents and Teachers :

The story of the Guru being called to Delhi by Aurangzeb may be told. The Guru instead sent his elder son Ram Rai and explain how the latter's behaviour there by misinterpreting the Sikh scripture displeased the Guru.

Guru Harkrishan

Guru Harkrishan is the eighth Guru of the Sikhs. He became Guru at the age of five. He was the youngest son of Guru Har Rai. Gurdwara Bangla Sahib is built at the place where the Guru stayed when he came to Delhi.

Hints for Parents and Teachers :

During his stay in Delhi he cared and cured many people who were suffering from cholera. Children should seek inspiration from such a young Guru in imbibing values of self-sacrifice, truthfulness and care for others.

Guru Tegh Bahadur

Guru Tegh Bahadur was the youngest son of Guru Hargobind. He is the ninth Guru of the Sikhs.

The Moghul king was forcibly converting the Hindu pandits of Kashmir to Islam. The pandits came to Guru Tegh Bahadur for help. He sacrificed his life to save their religion.

Hints for Parents and Teachers :

The story of Kashmiri *pandits* who came to seek his advice for being forcibly converted to Islam may be told. Also tell the story of his martyrdom. It may be emphasized that the Guru sacrificed his life to protect their religion.

Guru Gobind Singh

Guru Gobind Singh is the tenth Guru of the Sikhs. He was the only son of Guru Tegh Bahadur. He started the Khalsa order. He said that the Guru Granth Sahib will be the Guru after him.

Hints for Parents and Teachers :

The sacrifices made by Guru Gobind Singh, particularly the sacrifice of his four sons, will be of interest to the children. The story of the founding of the Khalsa order in 1699 may be told.

Guru Granth Sahib

Guru Granth Sahib is the holy book of the Sikhs. It was compiled by Guru Arjan Dev. It has writings mainly of the Sikh Gurus, and some of Muslim fakirs and Hindu saints. Guru Gobind Singh said that this holy book shall be the Guru after him. It is kept in all gurdwaras.

Hints for Parents and Teachers :

Tell the children that there is no living Guru after Guru Gobind Singh. Holy book—Guru Granth Sahib— containing "Gurus' word" is the only eternal Guru of the Sikhs.

THE SIKH SHRINES
Gurdwara

A Sikh temple is called a gurdwara. Guru Granth Sahib is kept here. It is a place of worship but not of idol worship. A gurdwara can be known from a distance by the tall Nishan Sahib. Langar is served in most gurdwaras. They are open to all. Many Sikhs have private gurdwaras in their homes.

Hints for Parents and Teachers :

Children should be told about the significance of a gurdwara as a place for religious and social functions. Concepts of *Charhawa*, *prasad*, voluntary service of cleaning the premises, keeping shoes and community kitchen-*langar*, may be brought out. The idea of humility and equality behind these concepts should be stressed.

The Golden Temple

The Golden Temple is the most important gurdwara for the Sikhs. It was built by Guru Arjan Dev. It is in Amritsar. It is called the Golden Temple because of the gold plating done on it. It is also called Harmander Sahib or Darbar Sahib.

Hints for Parents and Teachers :

Tell children that Golden Temple is the most holy and chief shrine for the Sikhs. It is built in the middle of a square tank. Also mention that the foundation stone was laid by a Muslim saint. Many Hindus visit it. It has four doors—one in each direction—indicating that it is open to all.

The Akal Takhat

Among the gurdwaras, some have special importance for the Sikhs. They are called Takhats meaning thrones. There are five such Takhats. Akal Takhat is the oldest and the first Takhat. It is inside the Golden Temple complex in Amritsar. It was built by Guru Hargobind.

Takhat Keshgarh Sahib

Keshgarh Sahib is a very important gurdwara at Anandpur Sahib in Punjab. This is the place where Guru Gobind Singh had started the Khalsa order.

Hints for Parents and Teachers :

Children should be told the story of the creation of the Khalsa brotherhood by Guru Gobind Singh on the Baisakhi of 1699 A.D., explaining the *Panj Piaras* and the five K's.

Takhat Sri Harmander Sahib

Sri Harmander Sahib is a very important gurdwara in Patna, Bihar. It is the birth place of Guru Gobind Singh.

Hints for Parents and Teachers :

Tell the children that important places of Sikhs are not confined to Punjab alone. Also tell some stories about Guru Gobind Singh's childhood.

Takhat Hazur Sahib

Hazur Sahib is a very important gurdwara in the city of Nanded in Maharashtra. Guru Gobind Singh died here. It was here he passed permanent Guruship to Guru Granth Sahib before his death.

Hints for Parents and Teachers :

Tell the story of how hired Pathans stabbed Guru Gobind Singh. Also tell his meeting with Banda Singh Bahadur here as well as how he declared Guru Granth Sahib as the eternal Guru after him.

Takhat Damdama Sahib

It is situated at village Talwandi Sabo in Punjab. Guru Gobind Singh stayed here for nearly a year and prepared the revised version of the Guru Granth Sahib which is now the eternal Guru of the Sikhs.

THE SIKH SYMBOLS
Ik Onkar

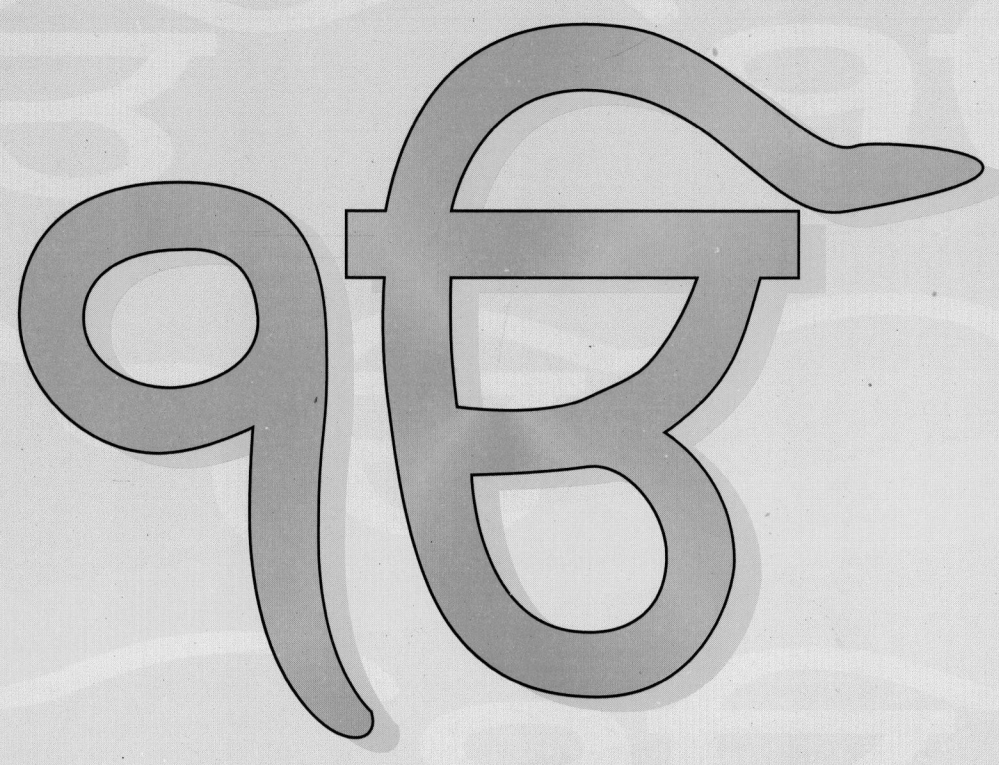

Ik Onkar is an important symbol of Sikhism. It is the first word of Mool Mantar in the beginning of Guru Granth Sahib. It gives the concept of God as one.

Hints for Parents and Teachers :

The children should recite *Mool Mantar* and explain to them the other attributes of God.

The Khanda

The Khanda is the emblem of the Khalsa. It has the following three parts:

1. Two-edged sword at the centre. This itself is known as Khanda.
2. Chakkar (an iron ring)
3. Two swords on either side of the Chakkar.

Hints for Parents and Teachers :

Explain the significance of the various components of the Khanda. The two edged sword symbolizes disintegration of false pride and inequalities. Chakkar exhorts the Sikhs to serve the whole creation. The two swords represent *meeri* and *peeri*.

Five Kakaars

The five symbols of the Sikhs are called Kakaars. Guru Gobind Singh said that every Sikh must wear these. They are known as Kakaars because their names begin with K. They are :

1. Kesh   : Uncut hair
2. Kara   : Iron bangle
3. Kangha : Comb
4. Kirpan : Sword
5. Kachha : Drawers or short pants

Hints for Parents and Teachers :

Tell the children that five K's are the mark of identity and belongingness to the Khalsa order.

Nishan Sahib

Nishan Sahib is the name given to the flag of the Khalsa. It is saffron in colour, triangular in shape and the Khanda in black. The flag post is generally covered with a saffron cloth and has a metallic Khanda at the top. The Nishan Sahib is installed in every gurdwara.

THE SIKH PERSONAGES
Panj Piare

Guru Gobind Singh started the Khalsa order on the Baisakhi day of the year 1699. He chose the first five Sikhs among the people who had assembled on that day. They were given amrit and named Panj Piare – the five loved ones. They were: Daya Ram, Dharam Das, Mohkam Chand, Sahib Chand and Himmat Rai. Now the term is used for any five devout Sikhs leading a procession.

Hints for Parents and Teachers :

Tell the story as how *Panj Piare* were selected and the Guru then took *amrit* from them and his name was changed from Gobind Rai to Gobind Singh and of Panj Piare to Daya Singh, Dharam Singh, Mohkam Singh, Sahib Singh and Himmat Singh. They were given special form by wearing five *kakaars* and it was ordained that the names of all Sikh men must end with "Singh" (Lion) and of the women with "Kaur" (Princess).

Char Sahibzade

Four sons of Guru Gobind Singh are affectionately called Char Sahibzade. They are remembered every time Ardaas is said. This is because they sacrificed their lives for the cause of Sikhism.

Sahibzada Fateh Singh

Sahibzada Zorawar Singh

Sahibzada Fateh Singh was 6 years old and **Sahibzada Zorawar Singh** was 8 years old when on their refusal to be converted to Islam, they were martyred in Sirhind.

Sahibzada Jujhar Singh

Sahibzada Ajit Singh

Sahibzada Jujhar Singh was 14 years old and **Sahibzada Ajit Singh** was 18 years old when they sacrificed their lives fighting in the battle of Chamkaur against the oppressive forces of Mughal ruler.

Hints for Parents and Teachers :

Talk about the sacrifices made by Guru Gobind Singh for Sikhism. Also recount how bravely elder Sahibzadas fought at Chamkaur Sahib and how resolutely the younger ones refused to be converted to Islam.

THE SIKH PRACTICES
Paath

Paath means recitation or reading of Gurbani from Guru Granth Sahib.

Akhand Paath means the recitation of the entire Guru Granth Sahib without any break. It takes about 48 hours to do so. It ends with Ardaas and then Karah Prasad is distributed.

Hints for Parents and Teachers :

Significance of *Paath* and the status of the Guru Granth Sahib may be brought out. Children may also be told about the important occasions when Akhand Paath is organised.

Shabad Kirtan

Shabad Kirtan is the singing of hymns from the Guru Granth Sahib. Generally Guru Granth Sahib is present at the time of Shabad Kirtan. Shabad Kirtan is a part of most of the religious ceremonies of the Sikhs.

Hints for Parents and Teachers :

At this stage, children must know the discipline of participating in it by taking off shoes, covering one's head, sitting on the floor facing Guru Granth Sahib and listen quietly the *Kirtan* which is *Shabad* of the Guru.

The Ardaas

The Ardaas is the common prayer of the Sikhs. It is usually recited at the beginning and at the end of an important occasion. This is a way of remembering God, the Gurus and the sacrifices made by Sikhs in history.

Hints for Parents and Teachers :

Though written by Guru Gobind Singh and later expanded by Bhai Mani Singh, further additions have been made by edicts of the Akal Takhat. Thus the *Ardaas* seems to encapsulate the on-going history and unity of Sikhs. Important occasions when the *Ardaas* is recited should be made known to the children.

Langar

Langar is the free community kitchen. It is an essential part of gurdwaras today. Uncooked food items are bought from the contributions of all. Food is cooked by volunteers. It is served to people of all castes, religions—both rich and poor, sitting together in a row. Guru Nanak Dev started this practice. It was carried on by other Gurus.

Hints for Parents and Teachers :

The children may be introduced to the fact that in Sikh religion there is no caste system. The concepts of equality, sharing and charity may also be emphasised at this point.

Dastaar Bandi

The ceremony of tying a turban to the male child is called Dastaar Bandi. This ceremony is performed at a gurdwara or at home in the presence of Guru Granth Sahib. For Sikhs the turban is a part of their dress because it serves as a protection for the Kesh (hair) on the head and it gives special form to the Sikhs.

The Sikh Salutation

The Sikhs greet each other with folded hands and say: Sat Sri Akal, which means: The God is Truth.

Guru Gobind Singh had earlier prescribed the greeting:

"Waheguru ji ka Khalsa; Waheguru ji ki Fateh." –Which means:

The Khalsa belongs to God; victory also belongs to Him. This form of greeting is still used by devout Sikhs and in religious functions.

Hints for Parents and Teachers :

Tell the children that after the martyrdom of Banda Bahadur the war cry of the Sikhs became "*Jo Bole so Nihal, Sat Sri Akal.*"

THE SIKH FESTIVALS
Gurpurab

Gurpurab is a celebration of the birth or death anniversary of Gurus. The birthdays of Guru Nanak Dev and Guru Gobind Singh and the martyrdom day of Guru Arjan Dev and Guru Tegh Bahadur are celebrated by the Sikhs on a big scale all over the world. Celebrations consist of Akhand Paath, Shabad Kirtan, Procession and Langar.

Hints for Parents and Teachers :

Experience of participating in *gurpurab* celebrations is very important. Children should be made to undergo all aspects of the celebrations as soon as possible.

Baisakhi

Baisakhi is the traditional north Indian harvest festival. It was celebrated even before the days of Guru Nanak Dev.

It was on the Baisakhi day in the year 1699. that Guru Gobind Singh started the Khalsa Panth. Since then Baisakhi has got a very special importance for the Sikhs.

Hints for Parents and Teachers :

Tell the children that it is the birthday of the Khalsa. Also explain the association of Bhangra dance with this festival.

Hola Mohalla

Holi is a Hindu festival when people sprinkle coloured water on each other. Guru Gobind Singh instead made it an occasion for Sikhs to show their marshal skills by mock battles, archery and wrestling contests. He named this festival as Hola Mohalla. The first Hola Mohalla was organised by Guru Gobind Singh at Anandpur Sahib in the year 1701.

The above pattern of celebrations has continued upto the present times. Thousands of Sikhs visit Anandpur Sahib on this day. The culmination is a grand procession.

Hola Mohalla always falls on the day following Holi.

Hints for Parents and Teachers :

Mythological basis for the celebration of Holi by the Hindus may be explained.

Diwali

Diwali's association with Sikhs started when Guru Amardas asked the Sikhs to come to Goindwal on every Diwali and Baisakhi. Also in the year 1597, the construction of the Golden Temple was started on the Diwali day.

Most importantly Diwali is celebrated by the Sikhs to mark the release of Guru Hargobind from the Gwalior fort in the year 1619. After the release Guru Hargobind arrived in Amritsar on the Diwali day and the Golden Temple was illuminated. The tradition has since been continued upto the present times. Now the fireworks and lights are displayed at Golden Temple and other gurdwaras.

Sikhs do not indulge in any special worship of idols or money on this day. They however display lights at their homes and exchange gifts.

Hints for Parents and Teachers :

Explain the Hindu mythology on which the celebration of Diwali among the Hindus is based. Sikhism being against gambling which is common on Diwali, must be emphasized.

QUIZ ON SIKHISM

THE SIKH GURUS

1. Who is the founder of Sikhism ? ....
2. Who founded the city of Amritsar ?.............................
3. Who got the Guru Granth Sahib compiled ?

   ....

4. Who started the construction of the Golden Temple ?...
5. Who built the Akal Takhat ?....................................
6. Who was the last living Guru of the Sikhs ?
7. Name the sixth and eighth Guru of the Sikhs.

   ....

8. Who started the Khalsa Panth ?...............................
9. Who is the present Guru of the Sikhs ?.......................

THE SIKH SHRINES

1. Mention one important feature of a *gurdwara*.

   ....

2. Give two other names by which the Golden Temple is referred to in common speech. .... , ...
3. Why is it called Golden Temple ?..............................
4. Name the five Takhats. .... , ...

   .... , ... , ...

5. Can Muslims and Christians visit *gurdwaras* ?

   ....

THE SIKH SYMBOLS

1. What does the expression *Onkar* mean ?

   ....

2. Name the weapons which constitute the emblem of *Khanda.* ....

3. Name the five *Kakaars.* ....

4. Which Guru gave us the five *Kakaars* ? ....

5. What is the shape of the *Nishan Sahib* ?........................

6. What is at the top of the flag post of the *Nishan Sahib* ?

   ....

7. What is the colour of the *Nishan Sahib* ?........................

8. Where do you generally see a *Nishan Sahib* fluttering high in the air ?..

THE SIKH PERSONAGES

1. Give the names of five first *Panj Piare*.

   .... ,............. , ... , ... , ...

2. Name the four Sahibzadas in order of age.

   .... ,.............................. ,.............................. ,

3. Which Sahibzadas died fighting in the battle of Chamkaur ? .... , ...

4. Name the Sahibzadas who were martyred in Sirhind.

   .... , ...

SIKH PRACTICES

1. How long the *Akhand Path* takes to complete ?..............

2. What is Shabad Kirtan ? ....

3. What is the name of the prayer of the Sikhs ?.................

4. Can low-caste people of whatever community partake food at a *langar* ?...

5. Give two important features of *langar*.

   ....

6. At what age a Sikh boy starts wearing a turban ?............

7. How do Sikhs greet when meeting each other ?

   ....

THE SIKH FESTIVALS

1. Name one *Gurpurab* in which you have or you would like to participate. ....

2. Give two most important features of Gurpurab celebrations. ....

3. Why Baisakhi has special importance for the Sikhs ?

   ....

4. Who organised the first Hola Mohalla at Anandpur Sahib?..

5. Do Sikhs throw coloured water while celebrating Hola Mohalla? ....

6. Hola Mohalla falls before or after Holi ? ....

7. The building of Golden Temple was started on which day?...

8. How is Diwali associated with Guru Hargobind ?

   ....

9. Do Sikhs worship idols or money on Diwali day ?

   ....

10. Are Sikhs supposed to gamble ?.....................................